As we move forward into this new age of AI-enhanced creativity, the possibilities are endless. The tools at your fingertips today are more powerful than ever before, giving you the ability to create, explore, and collaborate in ways that would have been unimaginable just a few decades ago. Whether you're an artist, musician, or writer, you have the opportunity to push the boundaries of your craft, to experiment with new ideas, and to redefine what it means to be creative.

AI is not here to replace you—it is here to inspire you. It can handle the technical aspects, it can suggest new possibilities, but it is your vision, your emotion, and your intuition that will give these creations their soul. As we enter this new Renaissance, the question is not whether AI can be creative, but how you will use it to unlock your own creativity.

This is your creative revolution—what will you do with it?

*Jaxon Steele*

# Introduction: The Intersection of AI and Creativity

In every age, creativity has been at the heart of human progress. From the first cave paintings to the latest digital art installations, humans have used creative expression to explore the world around them, communicate complex emotions, and shape culture. Creativity is, in many ways, what makes us uniquely human—it's the ability to imagine, to bring something entirely new into existence. But what happens when machines—those cold, logical entities born from silicon and code—begin to create? What does it mean when artificial intelligence starts composing symphonies, painting portraits, or writing novels?

We are standing at a fascinating crossroads in the evolution of art and technology. In recent years, artificial intelligence (AI) has advanced to the point where it can now generate artwork, music, and literature that, at times, is indistinguishable from human creations. Tools like DALL·E can take a text prompt and turn it into a surreal painting; platforms like AIVA can compose an entire orchestral score in minutes; and language models like GPT-3 can craft coherent, sometimes even poetic, narratives. These technologies are not merely assisting humans in creative tasks; they are producing original content that challenges our understanding of creativity itself.

But as we embrace these new tools, we are also confronted with deep and unsettling questions. Can AI truly be creative, or is it simply mimicking the patterns of human creativity? Is a painting created by an algorithm as valuable as one painted by a human hand? Can an AI-composed symphony stir the same emotions as a piece written by a composer who has lived through love, loss, and joy? These questions force us to reconsider our definitions of art, authorship, and the role of technology in human expression.

At the same time, AI is democratizing creativity in unprecedented ways. Artists, musicians, and writers who might have once been limited by technical skills or resources now have access to powerful tools that can assist them in bringing their visions to life. An artist with no formal training in painting can use AI to create a masterpiece. A filmmaker with a limited budget can use AI-driven cameras and editing software to produce professional-quality films. A writer struggling with writer's block can turn to AI for inspiration or structure. In this sense, AI is not replacing human creativity—it is amplifying it, allowing more people to participate in the creative process than ever before.

And yet, there are limitations. As sophisticated as AI-generated art and music may seem, there is still something deeply human about creativity that machines cannot replicate. Creativity, for humans, is often born out of struggle, emotion, and experience. A painter doesn't just paint a landscape—they paint the way the landscape makes them feel, the way it connects to a memory, a moment of joy, or sorrow. A composer writes a symphony not just to fill the air with sound, but to express the complexities of their inner world, to communicate something that words cannot. Can a machine, devoid of emotion, personal experience, and consciousness, ever truly create in the way a human does?

This book explores these questions and more. It is a journey into the heart of AI and creativity, an examination of how AI is transforming the fields of visual art, music, and writing, and a reflection on what these changes mean for the future of human expression. Along the way, we will look at the tools and technologies that are driving this revolution, from AI-powered content creation platforms to machine learning algorithms capable of producing entire works of art. We will dive into the philosophical debates surrounding AI's role in creativity, asking whether machines can ever truly be creative or if they will always be limited to imitation and assistance.

But this book is not just about the technology. It is about the symbiotic relationship between humans and machines. While AI may never feel the same emotions that drive human creativity, it can still act as a powerful partner—an assistant that helps us push the boundaries of what we can imagine and create. AI can handle the technical aspects of art, music, and writing, freeing human creators to focus on conceptual innovation, emotional expression, and cultural significance.

As we stand on the brink of this new creative frontier, it is important to remember that creativity is not a zero-sum game. The rise of AI in creative fields does not signal the end of human creativity; rather, it opens up new possibilities. Just as the invention of the camera changed the way we think about painting, and the advent of digital music transformed the recording industry, AI is simply the next evolution in the tools we use to express ourselves. And like those previous innovations, AI will challenge us, inspire us, and push us to rethink what it means to be creative.

So, can AI be creative? Yes, but with caveats. AI can generate art, music, and stories, but the true creativity lies in how humans use these technologies. We are still the ones who shape the narrative, who breathe life into the work, who give it meaning. AI is a tool—an extraordinarily powerful one—but it is still up to us to decide what to create with it.

This is a book for artists, musicians, writers, and creators of all kinds. It is for those who are curious about how technology is transforming the creative process and for those who wonder what the future of creativity might hold. In the chapters that follow, we will explore the tools and techniques that are at the forefront of this revolution. We will look at the ways AI is being used in visual art, music, and writing, and we will dive into the ethical, cultural, and philosophical questions that arise when machines enter the creative arena.

At its core, this book is an invitation to imagine—a chance to consider how human creativity and artificial intelligence might come together to shape the art, music, and literature of the future. As we explore this intersection of AI and creativity, let us embrace both the challenges and the possibilities, knowing that the heart of creativity will always remain, at least in part, uniquely human.

# Chapter 1: AI in Visual Art: From Pixel to Paintbrush

"Art is the lie that enables us to realize the truth."
**– Pablo Picasso**

Art has always been a reflection of the human soul—a way to capture fleeting moments of emotion, to make sense of the world, and to express ideas that cannot be easily conveyed with words. From the cave paintings of Lascaux to the abstract masterpieces of Picasso, art has evolved with humanity, often pushed forward by new tools and technologies. Today, we stand at the dawn of a new artistic revolution: one in which artificial intelligence holds the paintbrush.

AI is no longer limited to logical calculations or data analysis. In recent years, AI has entered the world of visual art with tools capable of generating original images, paintings, and even digital masterpieces that blur the line between human creativity and machine intelligence. But can a machine truly create art? And if so, what does that mean for the future of human artists?

**The Rise of AI in Visual Art**

Imagine a blank canvas, not held by a human hand, but by an algorithm—an artificial intelligence system that has been trained on thousands, or even millions, of images from various artistic styles. From abstract expressionism to classical realism, AI can study the intricate patterns, textures, and techniques of history's greatest artists, and then use this knowledge to produce something entirely new. This is the world of AI-generated art.

One of the most well-known AI tools in this realm is DALL·E, an AI model developed by OpenAI that can generate highly detailed images from simple text prompts. Users can input phrases like "a surreal landscape with floating islands and waterfalls" or "a cat dressed as an astronaut in a cosmic forest," and within seconds, DALL·E produces a visual representation of those ideas. The results can be striking—sometimes bizarre, often beautiful—and always surprising. These images are not copies of existing artwork but original creations, born from the AI's ability to combine various elements and styles.

Another example is DeepArt, an AI system that applies the artistic style of one image (such as a painting by Van Gogh) to another image, creating a fusion of styles. Through a process known as neural style transfer, DeepArt can take a photograph and render it in the style of a famous painting, making it look as though the scene was painted by the hand of a master. The result is a stunning combination of classic and contemporary, human and machine.

But perhaps the most famous AI-generated artwork to date is Portrait of Edmond de Belamy, created by an AI trained by the Paris-based art collective Obvious. The portrait, which depicts a blurry, slightly eerie image of a man in a black coat, was generated using a Generative Adversarial Network (GAN)—a type of AI where two neural networks "compete" against each other to create increasingly realistic images. When the portrait was auctioned at Christie's in 2018, it sold for an astonishing $432,500, far exceeding expectations and sparking a debate about the nature of AI and art.

**Human vs. Machine in Art**

The success of AI-generated art raises a fundamental question: Can a machine truly be creative?

On one hand, the artwork produced by AI is undeniably original. It is not copying a pre-existing image, but rather synthesizing countless influences to create something new. However, critics argue that AI lacks the emotional depth, intentionality, and personal experience that are central to human creativity. For a human artist, creating a painting is often a deeply personal process, one that reflects their thoughts, feelings, and experiences. An AI, by contrast, is simply following algorithms—processing data, recognizing patterns, and producing an output based on its training. There is no emotion, no conscious intent behind the AI's creations.

In many ways, AI-generated art is like a mirror that reflects the data it has been trained on. It can mimic styles, evoke moods, and even surprise us with unexpected combinations of elements, but it lacks the inner world that human artists draw upon to create their work. This raises important philosophical questions about the nature of creativity. If creativity is defined by emotional expression and personal experience, then AI may never be truly creative. But if creativity is seen as the ability to generate new and innovative ideas—regardless of where those ideas come from—then AI may already be a creative force.

## AI as an Augmented Paintbrush

Rather than viewing AI as a competitor to human artists, many see it as a tool—an augmented paintbrush that allows artists to push the boundaries of their creativity. In the same way that the camera revolutionized painting, forcing artists to explore new styles and perspectives, AI is opening up new possibilities for artistic expression.

For example, ArtBreeder is a platform that allows users to create and manipulate images using AI. By combining elements of different images, users can generate completely new visuals—whether it's a fantastical landscape, a hybrid animal, or an abstract portrait. The AI serves as a collaborator, offering endless variations and possibilities that the human artist can then refine and shape. This collaborative process blurs the line between human creativity and machine intelligence, as the final product is the result of both human input and AI-generated output.

AI is also being used to assist with technical tasks that would otherwise take artists hours or even days to complete. Tools like Runway ML allow artists to generate special effects, remove backgrounds, and enhance images with just a few clicks. This not only speeds up the creative process but also enables artists to experiment with techniques and styles that may have been out of reach due to time or technical constraints.

While AI can handle the technical aspects of art, the human artist remains in control of the vision and concept. The artist decides what to create, selects the initial inputs, and makes the final decisions about the composition. In this way, AI is a powerful tool that extends human creativity, offering new ways to explore ideas and bring them to life.

### Case Studies of AI in Visual Art

As AI-generated art continues to gain popularity, we are seeing more and more examples of how this technology is being used in the creative world. One such example is the AI Art Gallery, an online platform that showcases AI-generated artwork from artists and technologists around the globe. The gallery features everything from AI-generated landscapes to abstract pieces, offering a glimpse into the future of art.

Another fascinating example is Refik Anadol, a digital media artist who uses AI to create immersive, data-driven installations. In his project "Machine Hallucination," Anadol trained an AI on millions of images of New York City, allowing the machine to "hallucinate" new images that blend architecture, nature, and abstract forms. The result is a mesmerizing, constantly evolving display that challenges our perceptions of reality and creativity.

In the world of fashion, AI is also making its mark. Robbie Barrat, an artist and programmer, used AI to create AI-generated fashion designs. Trained on thousands of images from fashion runway shows, the AI produces original clothing designs that are futuristic and avant-garde, blending textures, shapes, and patterns in ways that human designers may not have thought of.

These examples highlight the growing role of AI in the creative industries. Far from being a threat to human artists, AI is becoming a collaborator—an assistant that helps push the boundaries of what is possible in art.

### The Cultural Impact of AI Art

As AI-generated art becomes more prevalent, it raises important cultural and ethical questions. Who owns the art created by AI? Is the credit given to the machine, the programmer who designed the AI, or the artist who guided the process? These are questions that are still being debated, as AI continues to blur the lines between human and machine creativity.

There is also the question of value. Will AI-generated art hold the same cultural and monetary value as human-made art? While pieces like Portrait of Edmond de Belamy have fetched high prices at auction, there is still a sense of skepticism about whether AI-generated works can have the same emotional and historical significance as human-created masterpieces.

As AI continues to evolve, it will be fascinating to see how it shapes the future of visual art. Will AI-generated art be seen as a novelty, or will it become an integral part of the artistic landscape? Will human artists embrace AI as a tool, or will they resist it as a threat to their creative process? These are questions that we are only beginning to explore, but one thing is clear: AI is already changing the way we think about art and creativity.

**Real-Life Case Study: Portrait of Edmond de Belamy**

One of the most famous examples of AI-generated art is the Portrait of Edmond de Belamy. Created by the Paris-based art collective Obvious, the painting was generated using a Generative Adversarial Network (GAN), a type of AI where two neural networks compete to produce increasingly realistic images. The portrait sold at Christie's auction for $432,500, sparking conversations about the value of AI-created art and the boundaries of authorship. While the artwork was generated by the AI, the creative intent behind the project still came from the human collective, demonstrating that AI is both a tool and a collaborator in the creative process.

Try it yourself! Visit an AI art platform like **ArtBreeder** or **Deep Dream Generator** and experiment with creating your own piece of AI-generated art. Use a description from a dream, memory, or even an abstract idea and see how the AI interprets your vision. Once you have the result, reflect on how it aligns with your original concept. How does it feel to see your idea brought to life by an algorithm?

# Chapter 2: AI in Music: Harmonizing Code and Composition

"Without music, life would be a mistake."
**– Friedrich Nietzsche**

If visual art speaks to our sense of sight, then music speaks to our soul. The rhythms, harmonies, and melodies of music have long been intertwined with human emotion and experience, carrying the power to evoke feelings of joy, sadness, triumph, and nostalgia. From ancient folk songs to modern electronic beats, music has been an expression of cultural identity and individual emotion. But what happens when machines begin to compose? Can a code-driven algorithm write a symphony that touches the heart, or will it always lack the emotional depth that comes from human experience?

AI's foray into the world of music has opened up a new frontier for composers, producers, and musicians alike. With advanced algorithms capable of generating everything from classical compositions to pop songs, AI is quickly becoming a significant player in the music industry. But as with AI-generated art, the question remains: Can AI truly be creative when it comes to music, or is it simply following patterns and formulas?

## The Symphony of Code

Music is inherently mathematical. It's built on patterns, rhythms, and harmonies, which makes it an ideal candidate for artificial intelligence to step in and contribute. AI has been trained on vast databases of music, learning the structures of various genres—from jazz to electronic to classical—and then using that knowledge to generate original compositions.

One of the most prominent AI tools in music composition is AIVA (Artificial Intelligence Virtual Artist), a platform designed to compose classical music. AIVA is trained on the works of history's greatest composers, including Bach, Beethoven, and Mozart. By analyzing their compositions, AIVA can generate new pieces that are structured in a similar style, complete with intricate harmonies, counterpoint, and dynamic shifts.

But AIVA is more than just a replication of past music. It can create entirely new compositions by blending classical techniques with modern influences. Musicians and producers can use AIVA as a creative partner, inputting parameters like mood, tempo, and key to generate music that fits their specific needs. For example, if a filmmaker needs a melancholic piano piece for a scene, AIVA can produce a composition tailored to that emotional tone.

Another AI tool making waves in music is Amper Music, which allows users to create music quickly and easily by selecting the genre, mood, and instrumentation. Amper then generates a fully arranged piece that can be edited and customized by the user. This platform is especially popular in the advertising and video production industries, where background music is often needed on a tight deadline and budget.

What makes AI-generated music so intriguing is its ability to produce an infinite variety of compositions. Because AI can generate new combinations of notes, rhythms, and harmonies, the potential for musical creativity is vast. It allows musicians to explore musical ideas they may not have considered, providing a rich source of inspiration.

But while AI can mimic the technical aspects of music composition, the emotional dimension is where the question of creativity becomes more complex.

## AI as a Musical Partner

For many musicians, AI is not viewed as a replacement for human composers but rather as a collaborator. AI can handle the technical, repetitive, or time-consuming aspects of music production, freeing the human artist to focus on the emotional and conceptual elements. In this way, AI acts as an assistant, helping composers explore new ideas, generate complex arrangements, and streamline their workflow.

Take, for example, the legendary producer and musician Brian Eno, who has used AI-driven systems to create generative music—music that evolves and changes over time without human intervention. His 2017 album, Reflection, is a perfect example of this. The music is generated by algorithms, designed to continuously shift and transform, creating an ambient soundscape that never repeats. This kind of collaboration between AI and human artists opens up exciting possibilities for how music can be experienced, with each listener having a unique encounter with the composition.

Another intriguing example of AI in music comes from Sony's Flow Machines, which uses machine learning to generate pop songs. Flow Machines was trained on a vast database of songs from different genres, and in 2016, it helped create the world's first AI-composed pop song, titled "Daddy's Car"—a catchy tune that was made in the style of The Beatles. While the music was generated by the AI, a human musician was still needed to refine the lyrics and arrangement, highlighting how AI can assist but not fully replace human involvement.

This raises an important point: collaboration is where AI's real power lies in music production. Rather than trying to take over the creative process, AI offers musicians new ways to explore sounds, structures, and compositions they might not have discovered on their own. Musicians remain the driving force behind the creative direction, while AI provides a framework for experimentation.

### The Emotional Algorithm: Can AI Compose Emotionally Resonant Music?

One of the most significant criticisms of AI-generated music is its potential lack of emotional depth. Music has the unique ability to evoke powerful emotions, often connecting the listener to memories, experiences, or abstract feelings. Human composers draw from their own lives—their joys, pains, and triumphs—to create music that resonates on a deeply personal level. Can a machine, devoid of consciousness, replicate this emotional impact?

The answer is complicated. AI can certainly produce music that *sounds* emotional. By analyzing vast datasets of music, AI can detect patterns associated with specific emotions—minor keys for sadness, certain tempos for excitement, and specific chord progressions for tension. Using these patterns, AI can generate music that mimics the emotional tone of a piece written by a human composer. However, because AI lacks personal experiences, it doesn't *feel* those emotions—it simply calculates which musical elements are likely to evoke certain feelings in listeners based on previous data.

In this sense, AI-generated music may be emotionally evocative, but it lacks the personal touch of a human composer. While a human musician may write a piece inspired by a breakup, a moment of joy, or a profound sense of loss, an AI is simply following rules to produce a desired outcome. As a result, some argue that AI-composed music, while technically impressive, often feels mechanical or detached, missing the subtle nuances that come from human expression.

However, AI's ability to generate emotional music cannot be dismissed entirely. In some cases, AI has been used to create music that evokes genuine emotional responses from listeners. In the hands of a skilled human artist, AI can be a tool that enhances emotional expression, providing new ways to convey feelings and ideas through sound.

## The Role of AI in Music Production

Beyond composition, AI is also transforming the production side of the music industry. AI-powered tools are now being used to assist with mixing, mastering, and sound design, helping musicians and producers streamline the technical aspects of creating music.

For instance, platforms like LANDR use AI to automatically master tracks, analyzing the audio and applying the appropriate adjustments to optimize the sound. This process, which once required a trained sound engineer and hours of work, can now be completed in minutes. AI-powered mastering tools are especially useful for independent musicians and producers who may not have access to expensive equipment or the expertise of professional sound engineers.

AI is also being used to generate sound effects and ambient sounds for films, video games, and virtual environments. Tools like Endlesss allow users to collaborate in real-time, using AI to generate loops, beats, and melodies that can be built upon by multiple musicians. This ability to create music collaboratively, across distances, is changing the way we think about music production, opening up new possibilities for how music can be made and shared.

**Ethical Questions in AI Music**

As AI becomes more integrated into music production, it raises important ethical questions. Will AI replace human musicians and composers? As AI-generated music becomes more sophisticated, there is concern that machines could take over jobs traditionally held by human artists. If AI can generate high-quality music quickly and cheaply, will there still be a demand for human composers, especially in industries like advertising, video game scoring, and background music for film?

Another ethical consideration is authorship. If an AI composes a piece of music, who owns the rights to that composition? Is it the person who trained the AI, the developer who created the algorithm, or the machine itself? These questions are still being debated, as AI-generated content becomes more prevalent across creative industries.

**The Future of AI in Music**

Looking ahead, the future of AI in music production is filled with possibilities. As AI tools continue to evolve, we may see music that is personalized in real time, with algorithms generating music that adapts to the listener's mood, environment, or even biometric data like heart rate. Imagine a world where the music you hear changes based on your emotional state—AI could compose a custom soundtrack for your life, one that reflects your unique experiences and feelings.

At the same time, human musicians will continue to push the boundaries of what is possible with AI, using these tools to explore new genres, experiment with sound, and collaborate in ways that were previously unimaginable. Rather than replacing human creativity, AI will serve as a powerful tool that enhances the creative process, offering new opportunities for expression and innovation.

**Real-Life Case Study: AIVA and AI-Composed Symphonies**

AIVA (Artificial Intelligence Virtual Artist) is one of the leading AI platforms for composing classical music. Trained on the works of composers such as Beethoven and Mozart, AIVA creates original pieces that are both complex and dynamic. Many musicians use AIVA to generate new compositions, especially for background music in films and games, where the emotional tone needs to be set quickly and efficiently. However, while AIVA is proficient in creating technically impressive music, the emotional nuances—those slight variations that come from lived experience—remain the realm of human composers.

Compose your own piece of music using an AI tool like **AIVA** or **Amper Music**. Choose a mood, genre, or even a specific theme, and let the AI generate a composition for you. Once the music is ready, try adjusting the elements—change the tempo, add instruments, or tweak the arrangement. Does the AI's initial creation inspire new directions for your piece? How much of the final result feels like it came from you, and how much came from the AI?

# Chapter 3: AI in Writing and Storytelling: Crafting Tales with Code

"There is no greater agony than bearing an untold story inside you."
– **Maya Angelou**

Storytelling is one of humanity's oldest and most cherished forms of expression. From oral traditions passed down through generations to the written word's rise in books and now to multimedia narratives in films and video games, stories have always been our way of making sense of the world. They allow us to explore emotions, relationships, history, and even the unknown. But now, at the dawn of the 21st century, a new kind of storyteller has emerged—one that doesn't rely on lived experience or imagination: artificial intelligence.

AI has begun to infiltrate the world of writing and storytelling, offering new ways to generate content, assist with creative blocks, and even produce entire stories. But as with visual art and music, the presence of AI in writing raises profound questions about the nature of creativity, authorship, and the emotional depth of stories created by machines. Can a machine-crafted narrative evoke the same feelings of wonder, sorrow, or joy as a story written by a human hand? And what does this mean for the future of literature?

## AI-Powered Writing Tools: Automating the Creative Process

Artificial intelligence in writing has primarily taken the form of natural language processing (NLP)—algorithms that are capable of understanding and generating human-like text. At the forefront of this revolution is GPT-3 and its successors, which are designed to generate large amounts of coherent and readable text based on prompts provided by the user. These tools are already being used by authors, content creators, marketers, and businesses to write articles, short stories, blog posts, and even poetry.

For instance, GPT-3 can take a simple prompt like, "Write a story about a lonely robot on a deserted planet," and within seconds, it can generate a well-structured, coherent narrative complete with dialogue, character development, and a plot arc. This ability to generate creative content on demand is incredibly useful for brainstorming and idea generation. Writers often use AI-powered tools to help overcome writer's block, draft the skeleton of a story, or provide suggestions for improving tone, style, or pacing.

Tools like Sudowrite, built on similar AI models, take it a step further by offering specific suggestions for improving scenes or dialogue. A writer might input a scene where two characters are arguing, and Sudowrite will offer options for tweaking the dialogue to make it more emotionally charged or realistic. It can even provide alternative endings to a story, giving writers new perspectives and directions to explore.

While these tools are undoubtedly helpful, they raise an important question: Where does human authorship end, and AI assistance begin? If an AI suggests a major plot point or writes a large portion of a narrative, does the human writer retain full ownership of the story? Or should the AI be credited as a co-author? This question is becoming more relevant as AI-generated content becomes more sophisticated, and the lines between human and machine creation continue to blur.

**AI-Generated Fiction: Crafting Entire Stories**

The rise of fully AI-generated fiction is a fascinating and controversial development in the world of literature. While AI-assisted tools are helping writers refine and streamline their work, some platforms are generating entire stories from scratch. These AI-generated stories can range from short pieces to full-length novels, often without any human intervention beyond the initial prompt.

For example, AI Dungeon allows users to engage with AI to create interactive fiction. Players input commands, and the AI generates narrative responses in real time, shaping the story based on the user's choices. The AI draws from a vast database of text, constantly learning and adapting to create stories that feel dynamic and engaging. Although these stories are often rough around the edges, they offer a glimpse into a future where AI could generate complex, multi-layered narratives in a matter of seconds.

In 2020, GPT-3 was even used to write a short story that was published in the literary magazine Tor. The story, titled "The AI Who Loved Me," explored themes of consciousness and artificial intelligence—fitting topics for a narrative generated by a machine. While the story received mixed reviews, it demonstrated that AI-generated fiction can hold its own in human literary spaces.

But there is a difference between coherent and compelling. AI can generate text that makes sense grammatically and structurally, but does it have the same emotional depth, subtext, and resonance that human writers bring to their work? A human writer draws from personal experience, cultural context, and emotional insight to create stories that reflect the complexities of life. AI, by contrast, generates stories based on patterns and data without any true understanding of what it means to feel love, fear, or loss.

As a result, AI-generated fiction often lacks the kind of emotional weight that defines great literature. It may be clever, and it may be well-written, but it often feels mechanical, as if it's following a formula rather than exploring the full breadth of human experience.

## AI as a Collaborator: Augmented Storytelling

Despite these limitations, AI is proving to be a valuable collaborator for human writers, offering a new kind of partnership in the creative process. In this dynamic, the human author remains the primary storyteller, using AI as a tool to explore new ideas, refine their writing, or automate repetitive tasks.

AI can also help writers experiment with narrative structures and styles that they might not have considered on their own. For example, a writer working on a mystery novel might use AI to generate multiple possible endings, allowing them to explore different plot twists without having to manually write each one. Similarly, AI can suggest alternative character arcs or settings, giving the writer more options to choose from.

This kind of collaboration is particularly useful in genres like science fiction and fantasy, where world-building is a critical component of the storytelling process. Tools like World Anvil use AI to help writers create intricate fictional universes, complete with maps, political systems, and cultural histories. AI can generate detailed backstories for characters, suggest new elements to enrich the world, and even help ensure consistency throughout the narrative.

In this collaborative approach, the human writer remains in control of the story's emotional core, while AI assists in expanding the possibilities for plot development, pacing, and structural innovation. The result is a hybrid form of storytelling that combines the creativity of human experience with the analytical power of machine learning.

## The Limitations of AI in Writing

While AI is making significant strides in generating coherent and interesting stories, there are still key limitations that prevent it from fully replacing human writers.

One major limitation is the lack of true creativity. AI generates content by recognizing patterns in data—it learns from existing text and uses that knowledge to predict what comes next. But creativity, for humans, often involves breaking patterns, taking risks, and innovating in unexpected ways. Human writers don't always follow the rules of narrative structure or grammar; they bend them, subvert them, and sometimes even shatter them entirely to create something truly original. AI, however, is bound by the rules it has learned, which can make its stories feel formulaic or predictable.

Another limitation is the absence of personal experience. Human writers infuse their stories with their unique perspectives, emotions, and memories. A novel about love written by someone who has experienced heartbreak will carry a depth of feeling that an AI simply cannot replicate. AI lacks the ability to feel, to empathize, or to draw from real-life experiences, which means that its stories may fall flat when it comes to exploring the complexities of human relationships and emotions.

AI also struggles with long-term narrative coherence. While it can generate short stories or individual scenes with relative ease, AI often has difficulty maintaining consistency and thematic unity in longer works, such as novels. A human author understands how to build tension over the course of hundreds of pages, how to develop characters, and how to weave multiple plot threads into a satisfying conclusion. AI-generated stories, on the other hand, can become disjointed or meandering, losing focus over time.

**Ethical Considerations: Who Owns the Story?**

The rise of AI-generated fiction brings with it a host of ethical questions. If an AI writes a story, who owns the rights to that story? Is it the person who provided the prompt, the company that developed the AI, or the AI itself? These questions have significant implications for the future of authorship, intellectual property, and the publishing industry.

Currently, AI-generated content is treated as a product of the human who operates the machine. In most cases, the person who inputs the prompt or uses the AI tool retains ownership of the final work. But as AI becomes more autonomous and capable of generating complex narratives with minimal human input, this ownership model may be challenged.

Another ethical concern is the potential for plagiarism by proxy. AI learns by analyzing vast amounts of data, including books, articles, and stories written by human authors. In some cases, the AI may generate content that closely resembles existing works, raising questions about originality and copyright infringement. If an AI inadvertently produces a story that mirrors a published novel, who is responsible for the potential breach of copyright?

## The Future of AI in Writing

As AI continues to evolve, its role in writing and storytelling is likely to expand. In the future, we may see AI systems that are capable of generating entire novels or screenplays that are indistinguishable from human-written works. These stories could be personalized in real time, adapting to the reader's preferences, mood, or interests. Imagine a book that changes its plot based on the reader's emotional responses or a movie script that adapts as the audience watches.

AI may also play a larger role in collaborative storytelling beyond the individual author, influencing industries such as film, television, and video games. Writers' rooms may use AI as a brainstorming partner, generating dozens of possible narrative arcs or character developments for long-running TV shows. In video game design, AI could help create dynamic, evolving storylines that respond to player decisions in real time, offering a level of immersion that would be difficult for human designers to achieve alone.

As these technologies improve, we may see interactive AI-driven storytelling platforms where readers become part of the narrative, making choices that influence the direction of the story. AI could create entire worlds where each decision leads to a unique outcome, creating a personalized narrative experience for every user. This would take the concept of choose-your-own-adventure stories to an entirely new level, allowing for almost limitless possibilities in storytelling.

However, despite these exciting prospects, human creativity and authorship will remain at the center of writing and storytelling for the foreseeable future. While AI can assist in the technical and structural aspects of writing, it is still far from capturing the nuances of human emotion and the personal experiences that make great stories resonate with readers.

## Conclusion: The Role of AI in Augmented Storytelling

AI has undoubtedly made significant strides in the world of writing, offering powerful tools that assist authors in generating, refining, and expanding their creative works. These technologies have opened up new possibilities for storytelling, from interactive narratives to automated content generation, and they are helping writers push the boundaries of their craft.

However, despite the impressive capabilities of AI in text generation, it remains limited in its ability to create stories that capture the emotional depth, personal meaning, and cultural resonance that define human-authored literature. AI is a tool—one that can assist, inspire, and enhance, but not replace, the heart of storytelling: the human experience.

As we move further into the future of AI-driven storytelling, it is clear that the relationship between human creativity and artificial intelligence will continue to evolve. Writers and creators will find new ways to collaborate with AI, using these tools to explore fresh ideas, generate content more efficiently, and experiment with narrative structures. But at its core, storytelling will always be a profoundly human endeavor—one that AI can augment but never fully replicate.

## Real-Life Case Study: GPT-3 and AI Dungeon

GPT-3 is one of the most advanced natural language processing AI models, capable of writing coherent and creative narratives. In the interactive text-based game AI Dungeon, players input commands, and GPT-3 generates real-time responses, creating a dynamic and evolving storyline. This blend of AI and storytelling offers a glimpse into the future of interactive fiction, where the reader's decisions shape the narrative. AI Dungeon is popular not only for its storytelling potential but also for pushing the boundaries of what AI can achieve in real-time, participatory storytelling.

Use a tool like Sudowrite or GPT-3 to generate the beginning of a story. Start with a prompt or a brief description of a scene, and let the AI continue the narrative. After you have the AI-generated portion, take over and develop the story in your own voice. How does the AI's contribution influence the direction of your story? What parts of the narrative feel like they belong to the machine, and which parts resonate more with your personal style?

# Chapter 4: AI as an Assistant, Not a Creator: The Human Element

"The artist is nothing without the gift, but the gift is nothing without work."
— **Émile Zola**

As artificial intelligence continues to advance and make its presence felt in various creative fields, one thing has become clear: AI is an assistant, not a replacement for human creativity. In art, music, writing, and other creative disciplines, AI can offer powerful tools that enhance productivity, provide inspiration, and even expand the possibilities of what can be created. However, the emotional depth, intuition, and personal experiences that define creativity remain uniquely human.

## Augmentation, Not Automation

AI's role in the creative process is often misunderstood. There is a common fear that as AI becomes more sophisticated, it will replace human creators, making artists, musicians, and writers obsolete. However, this fear overlooks the fact that creativity is not a formulaic process that can be easily replicated by machines. While AI can assist with the technical and repetitive aspects of creation, the spark of human creativity—the ability to imagine, feel, and take risks—remains irreplaceable.

Take visual art, for example. Tools like DeepArt and ArtBreeder allow artists to experiment with new styles, generate countless variations of an image, and automate some of the more time-consuming aspects of digital art creation. However, these tools do not replace the artist's vision. The artist still decides on the initial concept, chooses the elements that make the final composition, and adds the emotional depth that turns a digital image into a piece of art.

In music, AI-powered platforms like AIVA and Amper Music can generate entire compositions, but it is the human composer who gives the piece its soul. AIVA might write a beautiful orchestral piece, but a human musician understands how to layer instruments, control dynamics, and add the subtle nuances that turn a collection of notes into an emotional journey. Even in writing, while AI tools like GPT-3 can generate coherent stories, it is the human writer who imbues meaning, context, and personal experiences into the narrative, creating stories that resonate with readers on a deeper level.

**The Power of Human Intuition**

One of the fundamental limitations of AI in creative fields is its inability to tap into intuition. Humans are often driven by a sense of instinct when creating something new. We make decisions based on our emotional responses, life experiences, and cultural backgrounds—elements that are deeply personal and difficult to quantify. AI, by contrast, lacks this intuition. It can analyze patterns, follow instructions, and generate content based on data, but it cannot feel. It doesn't know what makes a song heartbreaking, a painting profound, or a story inspiring. It simply follows the rules it has been taught.

Creativity often involves risk-taking and breaking the rules, which is something AI struggles with. A human composer might decide to add an unexpected chord progression, creating dissonance that resolves beautifully by the end of a piece. A painter might use unconventional materials or techniques to evoke a specific emotional response. A writer might craft a narrative that defies traditional structure, creating an avant-garde piece of fiction that resonates because of its uniqueness. These decisions are driven by intuition, something that cannot be coded into an algorithm.

**Creative Control: Who Holds the Reins?**

Another key aspect of creativity is control. While AI can assist in generating content, the human creator is still the one holding the reins. Artists, musicians, and writers are not simply inputting commands into a machine and passively accepting whatever it produces. Instead, they are using AI as a tool—selecting, refining, and shaping the output to align with their vision.

For example, an artist using ArtBreeder might generate dozens of variations of a portrait. They choose which elements to keep, which to discard, and how to tweak the final result to match their artistic intent. Similarly, a musician using Amper Music might generate multiple pieces of music and then decide how to arrange them, which instruments to emphasize, and how to blend the AI-generated elements with their own playing. Writers using GPT-3 might take an AI-generated draft and rewrite sections, infusing the story with their voice, style, and emotions.

The relationship between human creators and AI is therefore one of collaboration, not replacement. The AI provides suggestions, inspiration, and technical support, but it is the human who directs the process and makes the final decisions. Creativity is not something that can be outsourced entirely to machines. It remains a deeply personal, intuitive, and emotional endeavor, one that requires the human touch to be fully realized.

## The Ethical Dimensions of AI in Creativity

As AI continues to be integrated into creative fields, it raises important ethical questions. One of the most pressing concerns is the impact of AI on employment in creative industries. If AI can generate music, write articles, and produce artwork, will human creators still be needed? While AI has the potential to streamline certain tasks and reduce costs, it is unlikely to completely replace human creators. However, it may change the way we think about authorship, ownership, and the value of human creativity.

Another ethical consideration is the issue of authorship and credit. If an AI generates a piece of art or writes a story, who owns the final product? Is it the person who inputted the prompt? The developer who created the AI? Or is it the AI itself? These questions are becoming increasingly relevant as AI-generated content becomes more prevalent in industries such as advertising, publishing, and entertainment.

Furthermore, there is the question of bias in AI-generated content. AI systems are trained on data, and if that data contains biases—whether related to race, gender, or culture—those biases can be reflected in the AI's output. This is particularly concerning in fields like writing, where representation and diverse perspectives are crucial to creating stories that resonate with a wide audience. Ensuring that AI-generated content is free from bias and ethically produced is an ongoing challenge.

**Creativity in the Age of AI**

The future of creativity lies in the collaboration between human creators and AI. Rather than viewing AI as a competitor, we can embrace it as a tool that enhances our ability to create. In the same way that the camera changed painting, AI will challenge us to think differently about how we approach music, art, and storytelling. It will allow us to experiment with new forms, explore uncharted creative territory, and expand the possibilities of what we can achieve.

Ultimately, creativity is a human endeavor. AI can assist, automate, and enhance the creative process, but it cannot replace the emotional depth, intuition, and personal experience that define great art, music, and writing. In this new era of AI-enhanced creativity, the human element remains at the center—guiding, shaping, and breathing life into every creation.

Reflect on a project you've been working on—whether it's art, writing, or music. Try using an AI tool to help you develop one aspect of it. Let the AI offer suggestions, whether it's a new verse in a song, an alternative storyline, or an additional element in your art. Now, take a step back and analyze the results. How does the AI-enhanced version differ from your original? What role did the AI play, and how did it inspire you to take your project in new directions?

# Chapter 5: The Future of AI in Creative Fields – A New Renaissance

"The future belongs to those who
believe in the beauty of their dreams."
**– Eleanor Roosevelt**

The future of creativity is evolving faster than we could have imagined. With artificial intelligence becoming increasingly embedded in the processes of making art, music, and literature, the boundaries of what is possible in creative fields are constantly being pushed. As we peer into the future, we find ourselves at the dawn of a new Renaissance, one where AI doesn't replace human creativity, but transforms and expands it in profound and unexpected ways.

As we move forward, the symbiotic relationship between human creativity and machine intelligence will open new doors to artistic expression, enabling humans to create in ways we've never thought possible. This chapter explores the cutting-edge innovations on the horizon, the cultural and societal impact of AI in creative fields, and the exciting possibilities of AI-enhanced creative collaboration.

**Innovations on the Horizon: AI in Art, Music, and Writing**

As AI continues to develop, the tools and technologies we use for creating art, music, and writing will only become more powerful. Here are some of the innovations on the horizon that could redefine creative industries:

1. **Generative Art and AI-Created Worlds**: AI-generated art has already made waves, but the future will take it further. Artists could use AI to create entirely new visual worlds, populated with surreal landscapes, abstract designs, and evolving, interactive installations. AI's ability to process vast amounts of data and simulate natural patterns means that it could generate complex environments and creatures for use in digital art, gaming, and even physical installations.
   Imagine a museum exhibit where the artwork constantly shifts and changes, evolving based on the viewers' movements and interactions. AI could generate these environments in real time, creating experiences that are never the same twice. This opens the door to immersive, generative art that continuously transforms based on the input of its audience.

2. **AI-Driven Music Personalization**: Music is a deeply personal experience, and AI has the potential to make it even more intimate. We may soon see AI-driven music platforms that create personalized soundtracks in real time, adjusting based on the listener's emotional state, location, and preferences. For example, wearable devices that track your heart rate, mood, and physical activity could communicate with AI music generators, composing music that adapts to your environment and emotions.

   Imagine jogging through a park with music that swells in intensity as you pick up your pace, or sitting by a window on a rainy day while your playlist shifts to match the mood of the weather outside. AI-generated music could become an extension of your emotional landscape, providing a deeply customized auditory experience.

3. **Interactive and AI-Generated Literature**: We're already seeing AI tools assist writers in generating stories, but the future promises interactive, adaptive literature where the narrative evolves based on the reader's choices. With AI, stories could become more like collaborative experiences, where the reader is no longer a passive observer but an active participant

shaping the outcome.

AI could create stories that respond to the reader's preferences in real time, altering characters, settings, and plotlines based on the reader's input. Imagine a novel that adjusts its tone or direction depending on how fast the reader is turning the pages or the emotional feedback they provide. This fusion of AI and human interaction will create a new genre of literature where no two readers have the same experience.

4. **AI-Generated Films and Screenplays**: AI is already being used to help scriptwriters and directors generate ideas for film and television, but the future could see entire movies created using AI. While human directors will still oversee the creative process, AI could handle many technical aspects, such as generating scripts, designing scenes, and even creating digital actors.

   For instance, an AI could suggest different camera angles, visual effects, and scene transitions based on the mood and pacing of the film. Directors may collaborate with AI to create hyper-realistic visual effects, fully immersive 3D environments, and AI-generated characters that evolve as the story progresses. The seamless integration of AI into the filmmaking process will push the boundaries of what's possible in cinema, leading to films that are more immersive, visually stunning, and emotionally engaging.

## Immersive Storytelling with AI: A New Era of Narrative Experience

Perhaps the most exciting possibility for the future of AI in creative fields lies in immersive storytelling. With the rise of augmented reality (AR) and virtual reality (VR), AI will play a critical role in creating fully interactive narratives where the audience becomes part of the story itself.

Imagine walking through a virtual world where the narrative unfolds around you, with AI-driven characters responding to your actions in real time. These interactive story worlds could offer endless possibilities for personalization, with AI adjusting the narrative to reflect your decisions, emotions, and interests. In this kind of storytelling, the lines between creator and audience blur, allowing people to participate directly in the creative process.

AI could also create multi-sensory experiences, where the story is not just something you see or hear but something you feel. With haptic feedback, AI-generated soundscapes, and even scents and temperatures that change based on the narrative, the future of storytelling could become a full-body experience that immerses the audience in ways traditional media never could.

## AI as a Cultural Force: Shaping the Future of Creativity

The cultural impact of AI-generated art, music, and writing is already beginning to ripple through society, but its influence is set to grow even more profound in the coming years. As AI becomes more integrated into creative industries, we will need to grapple with how these technologies affect our understanding of creativity, authorship, and value.

One major cultural question is: What is the value of AI-generated creativity? While human-made art has always been valued for its emotional depth, personal narrative, and unique perspective, AI-generated content challenges these traditional notions. How do we assign cultural and monetary value to a piece of art or music created by an algorithm? Can AI-generated content have the same impact on society as a human-created masterpiece, or is it always destined to be seen as an imitation?

As AI-generated content becomes more prevalent, we may also see shifts in the creative economy. Artists, musicians, and writers will need to navigate a world where AI can produce content quickly, cheaply, and at scale. While this democratizes creativity—making tools available to more people—it also raises concerns about authorship and the future of creative professions. Will human creators still have a place in industries increasingly driven by AI, or will their role evolve into one of guiding, shaping, and interpreting AI-generated content?

**The Role of AI in Genre Evolution**

AI's ability to analyze and synthesize vast amounts of data from different genres means it could play a role in the evolution of artistic genres. By blending elements from various styles, AI can create hybrid forms of art, music, and writing that transcend traditional genre boundaries.

For example, AI-generated music might fuse jazz, electronic, and classical elements into something entirely new, creating genres that human composers may not have considered. Similarly, AI-written stories could combine science fiction with historical fiction or blend fantasy with detective noir, resulting in genre-defying works that challenge existing categories.

The evolution of genres is often driven by experimentation and rule-breaking, and while AI can sometimes struggle to innovate beyond the data it's been trained on, it may still play a critical role in pushing creative boundaries. By providing new combinations and possibilities, AI could inspire human creators to explore uncharted territory, leading to the birth of entirely new forms of creative expression.

## Towards a Symbiosis: The Future of Human and AI Collaboration

As we look ahead, the future of creativity will likely be defined by symbiosis—the collaboration between human creators and AI. Rather than replacing artists, musicians, and writers, AI will serve as a powerful tool that enhances human creativity. It will handle the technical tasks, offer inspiration, and suggest new possibilities, while humans remain at the helm, guiding the emotional, narrative, and conceptual aspects of the work.

In this collaborative future, AI will be seen not as a threat to creativity but as an extension of human potential. Creators will use AI to push the boundaries of imagination, exploring new forms, styles, and genres that would have been impossible without the assistance of machine intelligence. AI will free artists to focus on the emotional and conceptual aspects of their work, allowing them to express themselves more fully and authentically.

As we enter this new Renaissance, we must embrace the possibilities that AI brings while holding on to the core of what makes us human—our ability to feel, imagine, and create meaning. In the end, it's the human experience that will continue to drive the creative process forward, even as AI helps us realize our most ambitious visions.

# The Symphony of Human and Machine Creativity

As we reach the end of this journey into the world of AI and creativity, we find ourselves standing at the intersection of human imagination and machine intelligence, poised on the brink of a new creative frontier. The rise of artificial intelligence in art, music, and writing has sparked both excitement and debate, challenging our understanding of what it means to create and what role technology plays in the process.

Throughout this book, we've explored how AI is transforming creative fields, from generating visually stunning artworks and composing intricate musical pieces to assisting writers in crafting compelling stories. We've seen how AI can be a powerful collaborator, offering tools that streamline workflows, inspire new ideas, and push the boundaries of what is possible. But we've also examined the limitations of AI—its inability to feel emotions, its reliance on patterns and data, and its struggle to match the depth of human intuition and experience.

In the face of these challenges, one thing remains clear: AI cannot replace the human spark of creativity. It can mimic, assist, and enhance, but the emotional depth, personal narrative, and cultural resonance that define great art, music, and writing come from human experience. It is the artist's ability to feel, to imagine, and to take risks that infuses a work with meaning and allows it to resonate deeply with its audience.

## The Role of AI: Enhancer, Not Replacement

At its core, AI is a tool—one that can be used to amplify human creativity rather than replace it. Just as the camera changed the way painters approached their art, and synthesizers revolutionized the music industry, AI is simply the next evolution in the tools we use to express ourselves. It allows us to work more efficiently, to explore new forms of expression, and to experiment with ideas that might have been out of reach in the past.

In visual art, AI serves as a digital assistant, generating countless variations of a piece, suggesting new styles, and handling technical tasks that would otherwise take hours. Yet, the human artist remains the guiding force behind the work, making the final decisions and infusing the piece with emotional depth and meaning.

In music, AI can compose entire symphonies or suggest musical arrangements based on patterns it has learned from existing works. But it is the human composer who shapes the emotional arc, adds the subtle nuances, and understands how to connect with listeners on a deeply personal level.

In writing, AI can generate coherent narratives and provide valuable suggestions for structure and pacing. However, the human writer draws from their own life experiences, memories, and emotions to create stories that resonate with readers. It is this personal connection that gives stories their heart.

## AI and the Future of Creativity: Collaboration Over Competition

As we look toward the future, the relationship between human creators and AI will be defined by collaboration, not competition. AI will continue to evolve, offering new possibilities for artistic expression and creative innovation. But rather than replacing human creativity, AI will augment it, allowing us to explore new forms, genres, and styles that were previously unimaginable.

In the world of visual art, we may see artists collaborating with AI to create immersive, generative installations that change and evolve based on audience interaction. In music, AI may assist composers in crafting personalized soundscapes that adapt to the listener's emotional state or environment. In writing, AI could help authors create interactive narratives that respond to readers' choices, offering a personalized story experience for every individual.

The key to this future is symbiosis—a partnership between human creativity and machine intelligence. While AI handles the technical, repetitive, and data-driven aspects of creation, humans will remain the visionaries, guiding the process, infusing it with emotion, and shaping the final product. Together, humans and AI can achieve things that neither could accomplish alone.

## Ethical Considerations and the Value of Human Creativity

As AI becomes more integrated into creative fields, it raises important ethical questions about authorship, ownership, and value. Who owns a piece of art or music created by AI? Should the AI be credited as a co-creator, or does the credit belong entirely to the human who guided the process? These questions will become increasingly relevant as AI-generated content becomes more prevalent in industries like advertising, publishing, and entertainment.

Another critical question is: What is the value of human creativity in a world where machines can generate content quickly and cheaply? As AI becomes more capable of producing high-quality art, music, and writing, human creators may find themselves competing against algorithms that can work faster and for less money. This raises concerns about the future of creative professions and the role of human artists in an increasingly automated world.

However, human creativity remains irreplaceable. While AI can generate content based on patterns and data, it cannot replicate the depth of human emotion, the richness of personal experience, or the cultural significance that comes from living a human life. The value of human creativity lies not in its speed or efficiency but in its ability to connect us with each other, to express ideas and emotions that transcend time and place, and to create works that reflect the complexity and beauty of the human condition.

## The Eternal Dance Between Technology and Creativity

Technology has always played a role in shaping art, music, and storytelling. From the invention of the printing press to the rise of digital media, each new tool has challenged artists to think differently, to experiment with new forms, and to push the boundaries of their craft. AI is simply the latest step in this ongoing evolution—a tool that offers new possibilities for creative expression while raising new questions about the nature of creativity itself.

But throughout history, one thing has remained constant: The human spirit continues to drive the creative process forward. Technology may change the way we create, but it does not change the essence of creativity. It is still the artist, the musician, the writer who brings the work to life, who infuses it with meaning, and who connects it to the broader cultural and emotional landscape.

In the coming years, we will likely see more collaborations between humans and AI, with new forms of art, music, and storytelling emerging from this partnership. These creations will challenge our perceptions of what is possible, pushing us to rethink the boundaries of creativity. But at the heart of it all, human creativity will continue to be the driving force—using AI not as a replacement, but as a tool to enhance, inspire, and expand our creative horizons.

## A Creative Future: AI and the Human Experience

As we stand on the brink of this new creative era, it's important to remember that creativity is not a zero-sum game. The rise of AI in art, music, and writing does not mean the end of human creativity. Instead, it opens up new opportunities for collaboration and exploration. AI can take care of the technical and procedural aspects of creation, allowing human creators to focus on the conceptual, emotional, and intuitive dimensions of their work.

The future of creativity will be defined by hybrid forms, where AI and human intelligence work together to create something greater than the sum of their parts. Whether it's in visual art, music, writing, or storytelling, the relationship between AI and human creators will shape the creative landscape of tomorrow.

In the end, the question is not whether AI can be creative, but how we choose to use AI to enhance our own creativity. The symphony of human and machine creativity is only just beginning, and the possibilities are endless.

## Real-Life Case Study: Interactive AI and the Future of Immersive Storytelling

The future of storytelling lies in immersive experiences driven by AI, augmented reality (AR), and virtual reality (VR). One project leading the charge is Refik Anadol's Machine Hallucination. This installation uses AI to generate dreamlike environments by processing millions of photos of New York City. As the AI "hallucinates" new visual experiences, visitors are immersed in a continuously evolving narrative environment. Projects like this point toward a future where AI can create entire worlds, personalized to individual viewers and respond in real-time to their emotions and movements.

# Author's Reflection

As I sat down to write this book, I was filled with curiosity, excitement, and, if I'm being honest, a touch of uncertainty. The idea that machines—programs, algorithms, and lines of code—could assist or even participate in something as personal and profound as human creativity seemed almost too futuristic to grasp. But as I delved deeper into the world of AI and creativity, that uncertainty gave way to something else: wonder.

I've come to realize that AI is not something to fear, nor is it something that will diminish or replace what makes us uniquely creative. Instead, AI is a tool—one that offers us incredible new ways to amplify our imaginations, explore ideas, and bring our visions to life. It's not here to take over; it's here to partner with us. And what a powerful partnership it can be.

Let me say this clearly: **AI is here to stay!** It's already woven into the fabric of your daily life, from the recommendations you receive on streaming platforms to the virtual assistants that help you with everyday tasks. You're already consuming AI in subtle ways, and it's only going to become a bigger part of how we create and experience the world.

Think about it—we are on the verge of a new creative revolution. In the future, it won't be strange to see blockbuster films starring AI-generated actors, to hear platinum-selling AI musicians on the radio, or to read bestselling novels partially crafted by machine learning algorithms. There may even be award shows where AI-generated movies, art, and music compete alongside human-created works, not as novelties, but as legitimate contributions to culture. The possibilities are endless, and rather than being afraid of these changes, we should embrace them.

What AI does is give us more tools to work with. It can take on the technical tasks, it can generate infinite variations, and it can introduce us to unexpected creative possibilities. But what AI cannot do is replace the soul of creativity—the emotional depth, the personal experiences, and the unique perspective that only a human being can bring. The stories we tell, the music we compose, the art we make—all of that will still come from us. *AI enhances*; it does not replace.

In the hands of a visionary, AI is like a superpower. It extends your reach, expands your horizons, and allows you to build upon your own creativity in ways you never thought possible. It's like having a co-pilot who works tirelessly at your side, ready to suggest ideas, handle the technical details, and take your imagination to new heights.

As we move forward, there will be those who cling to the fear of the unknown, who worry that machines will one day make human creativity obsolete. But I'm here to tell you—that fear is unfounded. Creativity is evolving, not disappearing. And those who are willing to embrace AI as a partner, who are excited to experiment and collaborate with it, will find themselves at the forefront of this new creative Renaissance.

The world we are about to enter includes films that respond to your emotions in real time, music that adapts to your mood, and stories that change with every choice you make. Imagine artists co-creating with AI to make immersive installations that evolve and shift every time someone enters the room. AI alongside musicians composing symphonies, creating sounds and textures no one has ever heard before. That's the world that's coming—and you can be part of it.

So, don't be afraid. Use AI as your tool. Let it inspire you, let it challenge you, let it push your creativity in new directions. Because the truth is, AI isn't here to take away the magic of creativity—it's here to help you unlock even more of it.

The future of creativity is a beautiful collaboration between humans and machines, and I, for one, am excited to see what we'll create together. As you go forward, I encourage you to embrace this new era, to experiment fearlessly, and to use AI to amplify your voice, your vision, and your art. The future belongs to those who are willing to dream with both imagination and innovation. What will you create?

# Glossary of Terms

1. **AI (Artificial Intelligence)**: The simulation of human intelligence by machines, particularly computer systems, allowing them to perform tasks like learning, problem-solving, and creativity.
2. **Generative Adversarial Network (GAN)**: A type of AI where two neural networks compete against each other—one generating content and the other evaluating it for authenticity—leading to the creation of realistic outputs like images or music.
3. **Natural Language Processing (NLP)**: A field of AI focused on the interaction between computers and human language, allowing machines to understand, interpret, and generate natural language.
4. **Neural Network**: A series of algorithms that mimic the way the human brain operates, used in AI to recognize patterns, process data, and generate outputs in fields like image recognition, music composition, and natural language processing.
5. **Deep Learning**: A subset of machine learning based on artificial neural networks, which allows AI to process large amounts of data and learn from it without explicit programming.

6. **Machine Learning (ML)**: A branch of AI that allows systems to learn from data, improve their performance over time, and make decisions with minimal human intervention.
7. **Neural Style Transfer**: An AI technique that combines the content of one image with the style of another, often used to apply artistic styles (e.g., Picasso or Van Gogh) to photographs.
8. **Interactive Fiction**: A form of narrative where the reader or player makes decisions that affect the direction and outcome of the story, often powered by AI for real-time response.
9. **Augmented Reality (AR)**: Technology that overlays digital content on the real world, often enhancing storytelling and artistic experiences with interactive elements.
10. **Virtual Reality (VR)**: A fully immersive digital environment that users can interact with, often combined with AI to create responsive, adaptive narratives or artistic experiences.

# **Further Exploration**

For those who want to dive deeper into the world of AI and creativity, here are some resources to explore:

**AI Tools for Creativity:**

- **ArtBreeder**: A tool for creating and blending images using AI. Great for visual artists experimenting with styles.
  **Website**: artbreeder.com
- **AIVA**: An AI music composition tool that helps create orchestral pieces.
  **Website**: aiva.ai
- **GPT-3 / OpenAI**: A powerful language model that can generate text and assist with writing projects.
  **Website**: openai.com

**Courses on AI and Creativity:**

- **Coursera**: Explore AI and creativity through various courses, such as "Creative Applications of Deep Learning with TensorFlow".
  **Website**: coursera.org
- **Udemy**: Offers AI-focused courses in music production, art, and writing.
  **Website**: udemy.com

**Books and Documentaries on AI in the Arts:**

- **"You Look Like a Thing and I Love You"** by **Janelle Shane**: A fun exploration of how AI works and where it sometimes goes wrong, with examples from the arts.
- **"The Creativity Code: How AI is Learning to Write, Paint, and Think"** by **Marcus du Sautoy**: An insightful look at how AI is shaping the future of creativity.
- **"AI: More Than Human"** (Documentary): An exploration of AI's place in art, ethics, and society.
  **Available on**: YouTube or Vimeo

# Jaxon Steele: Empowering Minds in the Age of AI

Jaxon Steele is an educator, technologist, and futurist with a passion for exploring the cutting edge of artificial intelligence. With over a decade of experience at the intersection of education and technology, Jaxon is dedicated to helping teachers, professionals, and everyday individuals harness the transformative power of AI. His work bridges the gap between complex tech concepts and practical, real-world applications, making the future of AI accessible to all.

A thought leader in the field, Jaxon has consulted with educational institutions and businesses across the globe, helping them adapt to the rapidly evolving world of AI. His in-depth knowledge and hands-on approach provide readers with actionable strategies for thriving in an AI-driven society—whether it's personalizing the classroom experience, staying ahead in competitive industries, or simply understanding the everyday impact of artificial intelligence.

Driven by the belief that AI is not just a tool but an opportunity for growth, Jaxon has crafted the **AI Revolution Series** to empower others to embrace change and unlock their potential in the new tech era. With a unique ability to simplify advanced technology and inspire action, Jaxon Steele delivers insights that are as engaging as they are transformative.

When he's not writing or consulting, Jaxon loves to read and learn about new technology as well as spend time with his family.

Thank you for your purchase and be on the look out for more selections from Jaxon Steele! If you found this book helpful, I would greatly appreciate your review on Amazon. Your feedback helps me improve future content and ensures others benefit from this knowledge.

*Jaxon Steele*